The Monsters Visit Granny

Colin and Jacqui Hawkins

One Sunday morning all the monsters are reading their comics. Then the phone rings.

Yippee! Granny wants us to come and stay.
The monsters jump in the air with excitement.

They pack their cases and dash to the bus.

Hurry, hurry,' says Mummy pushing Baby monster even faster.

On the bus the monsters start waving and pulling funny faces at everyone.

Max sings silly monster songs at the top of his voice.

'Hello my dears,' Granny greets them all with a slobbery kiss.

'Aren't you a big monster!' says Grandad, throwing Max into the air.

'Let's have some tea,' says Granny.

They tuck into huge, sticky cakes.
'Yum, Yum, These are scrummy.'

After tea the little monsters rush off to play. Milly jumps on the swing. Wheee!

'I'm Tarzan,' yells Max.
Oh, what has Baby monster found?

The little monsters help Grandad in the garden.

Milly and Max race up and down while Baby monster waters the dog.

Rattle, clatter, crash! 'This is fun!' yells Max.

The little monsters love juggling with the plates as they help do the washing up.

That evening, Granny, who is a great knitter, gives them all a surprise.

'I don't like it,' cries Baby monster as Granny tries on his new bonnet.

After supper the little monsters play horsey, horsey with Granny and Grandad.

'Gee up, Granny. We've got to win,' shouts Milly.

'It's time for bed,' says Mummy monster.
'Goodnight Granny. Goodnight Grandad.'

Goodnight. Sleep tight,' but they are already fast asleep. Zzzzzz . . .

THE MONSTERS VISIT GRANNY

A PICTURE CORGI 0 552 523518
First published in 1984 by Beanstalk Books Ltd.
PRINTING HISTORY
Beanstalk Books publication 1984
Picture Corgi edition published 1986

Picture Corgi Books are published by
Transworld Publishers Ltd., 61-63 Uxbridge Road, Ealing
London W5 5SA
Printed by Purnell & Sons (Book Production) Ltd.